what we do

Hairdresser

JAMES NIXON

PHOTOGRAPHY BY BOBBY HUMPHREY

W

FRANKLIN WATTS

LONDON•SYDNEY

First published in 2012 by Franklin Watts

Franklin Watts
338 Euston Road
London NW1 3BH

Franklin Watts Australia
Level 17/207 Kent Street
Sydney, NSW 2000

Planning and production by
Discovery Books Limited
Editor: James Nixon
Design: sprout.uk.com limited
Commissioned photography: Bobby Humphrey

Dewey number: 646.7'24

ISBN: 978 1 4451 0888 9

Printed in China

Franklin Watts is a division of Hachette
Children's Books, an Hachette UK company.

www.hachette.co.uk

Acknowledgements: Shutterstock Images: p. 23
top (Losevsky Pavel).

The author, packager and publisher would like
to thank Remedy Hairdressing, Leeds, for their
help and participation in this book.

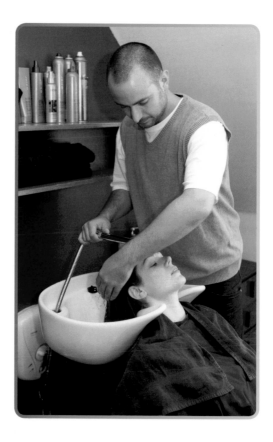

what we do

CONTENTS

Words in **bold** appear in the glossary on page 24.

I AM A HAIRDRESSER

My name is Hayley. I work as a stylist in a hairdresser's. This is our salon (right). The men have their hair cut downstairs. The women's section is upstairs. I cut and style both men's and women's hair.

The hairdressers in the salon work as a team to make sure the customers are looked after properly. The work is tiring. I spend most of the day on my feet, moving around different parts of the salon, washing, drying and styling hair.

▼ *We use a range of techniques to provide customers with the shape, colour and* **texture** *of hair that they want.*

There are a variety of brushes, scissors, products and other tools that I use to create different haircuts. Every customer's hair is different, but hairdressers know what styles and products are best for each person.

▲ *Chatting with the customers is a fun part of hairdressing.*

As a hairdresser it is important to form good relationships with your customers. You need to be friendly and chatty. My favourite part of the job is making people look good and feel happy about themselves.

KEY SKILLS

STAMINA – Even if you are tired and the salon is busy, you must be enthusiastic towards customers and do a neat job.

GREETING CUSTOMERS

Making customers feel comfortable while they are in the salon is as important as the haircut itself. When a customer arrives you need to give them a warm welcome.

Hairdressers must make sure that customers do not have to wait for long. Keeping the customers happy and satisfied will mean they come back to have their hair cut time and time again.

▲ *We help customers with their coats and bags and find a place for them to sit and wait.*

KEY SKILLS

FRIENDLY AND OUTGOING –
You need to have good people skills and the ability to put customers at ease. Many customers will want to have a chat.

When I am ready, I take a customer to a chair in front of a mirror and ask them what they want from their **appointment**. Do they want a simple trim or a full restyle? I have to listen well so I know exactly what they are looking for. Then I know that they will be happy with the end result.

▶ *During the consultation I find out what style will suit the customer best.*

At the reception desk I take payments and answer the telephone (left). Some customers ring up to book an appointment in advance. I write the time and date down in the book and whether they want a cut, colour or restyle. We will then make sure that there is a stylist available at that time.

CHOOSING A STYLE

Hairdressers give expert advice to customers when they are choosing a hairstyle. Sometimes I suggest ideas that the customer has never tried before. I choose styles and colours (right) that I think will suit the customer's type of hair and face shape.

Once a style is chosen, we wash the customer's hair at the basin. First, we test that the water is the right temperature. Then we cleanse the hair with shampoo by massaging it all the way through to the roots.

TOOLS OF THE TRADE

There are lots of different shampoos for different hair types. A shampoo for dry hair leaves an oily coating on the hair. If someone has greasy hair we use a shampoo that contains fewer oils.

8

KEY SKILLS

CREATIVITY – Hairdressers should be naturally creative and able to visualise if a change of hairstyle will suit the customer.

This is my colleague Nick (right) rinsing shampoo out before he conditions the hair to make it soft and shiny. **Conditioner** is rubbed into the tips of the hair, and then this is rinsed out as well.

Now the hair is ready to be cut. The customer is wrapped in a gown and a rubber collar is placed at the back of the neck, so they do not get covered in hair.

▼ *Nick places the rubber collar on to the customer's neck.*

CUTTING HAIR

Hairdressers use a variety of cutting techniques to create different hairstyles. A simple haircut called a bob is the same length all over. Layered hair is cut at different lengths overlapping each other.

A short back and sides is a popular style among men. To cut the top and sides we use a technique called club cutting. With club cutting, a section of hair is held out from the head and cut off at the tips (right). The sides are cut as short as possible and then this is merged to the top which is left a bit longer.

▼ *At the back of the head and around the ears, the hair is too short for a finger guide, so the scissors are used over a comb.*

ATTENTION TO DETAIL –
You need to have a steady hand
and be very precise.

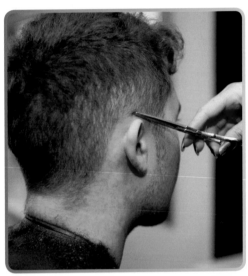

To neaten up the hairline at the top
of the neck and above the ear I use
the **clippers** (above) and the scissors
freehand (right).

Then to give the longer hair on
top some spikes or texture, I cut
it to different lengths by pointing
the scissors vertically over the
comb (below).

▶ *I always check that the customer is happy
with the result. They can see the back of their
head when I hold the mirror up.*

SHAPING THE HAIR

After the hair is cut, hairdressers blow-dry it into shape and use products to hold the hair in place. This is like the icing on the cake.

While drying, the hairdresser breaks the hair up with their fingers and angles it in the right direction. Then the hair is dried with special brushes to leave a smooth finish.

TOOLS OF THE TRADE

▲ *Nick uses an electric hand dryer in combination with a round brush.*

Round brush – To give hair extra lift, a round brush can be used while drying.

Vent brush – Hot air flows through the holes of this brush (right) to give shorter hair texture.

Diffuser – To dry long, wavy hair, a hair dryer attachment, called a diffuser, is used.

Once the hair is dry I can use electrical curling tongs to create waves or hair straighteners to remove unwanted curls. As a finishing touch I use hairspray to hold the hair in place. Sometimes I rub wax or gel evenly through the hair and pull it into shape.

▶ *Hair can be wrapped around straightening irons to produce neat curls.*

▼ *When I apply the hairspray I protect the customer's face with my hand.*

KEY SKILLS

PRESENTATION – In the beauty industry it is important to look good and keep yourself well groomed. The customers will then be confident that you will do a good job.

▶ *By rubbing wax into the hair I can create a spiky style which holds in place.*

GAINING EXPERIENCE

Trainee stylists learn the skills of hairdressing on the job. While they work, trainees also attend college to gain their professional **qualifications**.

This is our trainee, Miles (left). When a trainee position came up at the salon a friend told him about it. He had never considered hairdressing before but decided it was the right job for him. Miles goes to college once a week to do his National Vocational Qualifications (NVQs) in hairdressing. He has been here a year and in another year's time he will be fully qualified.

▶ *Miles sweeps the hair up when the customers leave.*

In the salon, trainees play an important part in looking after the customers as they arrive and wait. They also make sure that the salon is always kept clean and tidy. Miles is responsible for sorting out the fresh towels (right) and gowns. They need to be washed after each use.

Trainees assist stylists by carrying out less complicated jobs, such as washing customers' hair. They also observe and learn from the stylists at work.

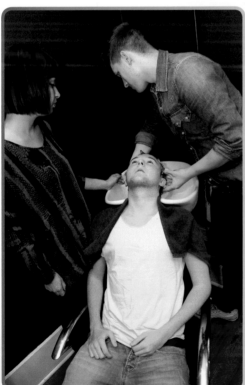

If you are applying for a trainee job it is useful to have some experience of dealing with the public, such as working in a shop. Good GCSEs in English and Maths, as well as Art to show your creativity, will also give you an advantage.

◀ *I help the trainees to learn. Here, I am making sure Miles washes the customer's hair correctly.*

KEY SKILLS

TEAMWORK – In a busy salon you need to work as part of a team.

COLOURING HAIR

Colouring hair requires advanced skills. You must understand how to use **tints** correctly to achieve the shade you want. You must also know how to work safely with **chemical** products.

▲ *Colour books*

I show customers a colour book to help them select a shade, and give them recommendations based on their natural hair colour. They can choose a permanent hair colour or a temporary colour that will come out when the hair is washed. Temporary colour **mousses** are scrunched into the hair using rubber gloves.

KEY SKILLS

FASHION CONSCIOUS – You need to have a keen sense of style and you need to keep up to date with the latest looks and trends.

When permanently coloured hair grows, the roots need redoing. This is Gerry (left). He is pasting tint on to a customer's roots with a brush. The tint is left on for 45 minutes and then rinsed off.

Bleach is used to lighten the colour of hair. Because bleach can be damaging to the hair we often use a highlighting technique. With highlights, only some strands of on the hair are coloured. I weave the strands of hair with a tail comb (below). Then I rest the hair on top of tinfoil and apply the tint with the brush (right).

TOOLS OF THE TRADE

When I have finished applying the colour, I sit customers under a special **infrared** heater to help the colour **penetrate** the hair.

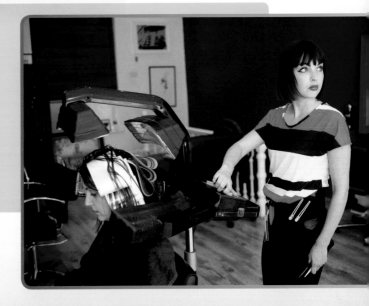

USING PRODUCTS

Hairdressers need an understanding of a huge variety of products. Once stylists are qualified they continue to build up their knowledge and stay aware of new products on the market.

Sometimes hairdressers attend short courses that introduce them to new products. The kinds of products available are changing all the time. Sales **reps** often pop in and talk to us about new items. It is important that we use and store products correctly.

▲ *Colours and **peroxides** have to be stored in a room where the temperature is cool.*

The chemicals in hair products mean that if you have skin problems, hairdressing may not be a suitable job for you. When a customer is having a tint for the first time I check that they will not have an **allergic reaction** to the product. I do this by testing a tiny amount on the inside of their elbow the day before their appointment.

Hairdressers must know which products can improve the look of different types of hair. For example, for fine hair, a stylist may use a dry mousse to give the hair extra **volume**. Here, Nick is working a gloopy, smoothing balm into the customer's hair to strengthen it (right).

▼ *Smoothing balms like this one make the hair strong and stop thick hair going frizzy.*

19

HAIR CARE

Hairdressing is also about helping customers keep their hair healthy. I give customers advice on how to treat any hair or scalp conditions they may have.

Before I cut hair I always analyse the customer's hair and scalp. I check for any hair problems that might need attention, such as **split ends** or **beaded hair**. For some scalp conditions, such as **psoriasis**, I might advise the customer to use a different shampoo. I also keep an eye out for any infections or **lice infestations**.

Hygiene is important so that infections are not passed on between customers. Brushes and combs are scrubbed to get the hair off and dipped into a disinfectant, called Barbicide, after every use (right).

▲ *I check the hair and scalp with a comb and keep an eye out for any lice.*

KEY SKILLS

GOOD COMMUNICATION – You need to be clear so that customers understand your advice.

◀ *Before every cut I wash my hands and rinse the Barbicide off the combs.*

There are certain hairstyling techniques where you have to be very careful not to seriously damage the hair. For example, putting in **hair extensions** is a delicate job which takes time. Small sections of hair are glued in with a sponge strip.

▼ *Hair extensions can transform a customer's appearance, but I must be careful that the glue does not damage the health of the hair.*

▲ *I advise my customers how to look after their hair extensions. If they brush their hair incorrectly they could fall out!*

GETTING ON

To become a qualified hairdresser you need to do *Level 1 and 2 NVQs in Hairdressing. Level 1* covers basic work, such as health and safety and shampooing. *Level 2* introduces you to cutting and colouring techniques.

KEY SKILLS

PASSION FOR HAIR – You must love the art of hairdressing and be willing to learn.

Here is my *Level 2* certificate (left). You can get your qualifications at college and then look for a job, or you can try to find work straight away as an **apprentice**. I was working as a waitress when I decided I wanted to be a hairdresser. Every night after work I popped into three or four salons and asked for an apprenticeship. By the end of the week a salon had offered me a job!

■ Hairdressers can find work in places other than salons. Hospitals, care homes, army bases and even cruise ships employ stylists. With experience you can progress to be a senior stylist or salon manager. *NVQ Levels 3 and 4* provide you with the skills to become a salon manager. Stylists can choose to become self-employed and open their own salon or work from home. Then they can work the hours that suit them. Top hairdressers can even go on to become stylists for celebrities or catwalk models (left)!

■ There are also opportunites for hairdressers to become expert in one particular area. For example, you could become a colour technician specialising in dyes. Some hairdressers go on to train as scalp problem experts while others become wig makers and fitters.

◄ *Hairdressers continually update their skills so that they can offer the latest styles.*

GLOSSARY

allergic reaction A damaging response by the body when it comes into contact with a substance.

appointment An arrangement to be somewhere at a particular time.

apprentice A trainee who learns the skills of the job as they work.

beaded hair Short, fragile, broken hair.

bleach A chemical used to make a material become white or much lighter.

chemical A substance used in chemistry which can be damaging to the skin.

clippers An electrical device for trimming hair.

conditioner A liquid applied to the hair to improve its condition.

freehand Without the aid of a guide.

hair extensions Strands of hair attached to a person's own hair to make it longer.

hygiene The practice of keeping yourself and your surroundings clean.

infestation The presence of something unwanted, in large numbers.

infrared A wave of light that is not visible to the human eye.

lice Wingless insects that infest the hair of humans.

mousse A light, foamy product that is applied to hair so it can be styled more easily.

penetrate To get deep into something.

peroxide A chemical mixture used as a bleach for the hair.

psoriasis A skin disease marked by red, itchy, scaly patches.

qualification A pass of a course or exam to show you are skilled at a particular job or activity.

rep A salesperson acting on behalf of a company.

split ends The tips of a person's hair which are split and damaged.

texture The feel and appearance of the surface of the hair.

tint A dye for colouring the hair.

volume Thickness of a person's hair.

INDEX